The Treasure of Trash
A Recycling Story

Linda Mandel
Hedi M. Mandel

Illustrated by Dick Codor

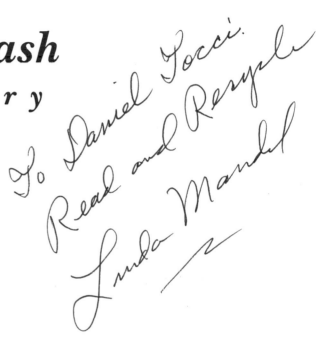

To Daniel Tocci,
Read and Recycle
Linda Mandel

AVERY PUBLISHING GROUP INC.
Garden City Park, New York

Cover Design: Dick Codor
Illustrations: Dick Codor
In-House Editor: Marie Caratozzolo
Typesetter: Bonnie Freid

Library of Congress Cataloging-in-Publication Data

Mandel, Linda, 1942–
    The treasure of trash : a recycling story / Linda Mandel, Hedi M.
  Mandel : illustrated by Dick Codor.
      p. cm.
    Summary: Explains how recycling and the conservation of natural
  resources can help save the Earth, with an emphasis on the recycling
  of plastic.
    ISBN 0-89529-575-X
    1. Plastic scrap—Recycling—Juvenile literature. [1. Plastic
  scrap—Recycling. 2. Plastic scrap—Environmental aspects.
  3. Recycling (Waste) 4. Refuse and refuse disposal.
  5. Environmental protection.] I. Mandel, Hedi M., 1967–
  II. Codor, Dick ill. III. Title.
  TD798.M36   1993
  363.72'82—dc20   92-41222
                                                      CIP
                                                     AC

Printed in the United States of America on recycled paper

10 9 8 7 6 5 4 3 2

To all the children of the world
and their adventure into recycling the planet
into a clean, healthy place.

This is the story of two families, the Apples and the Chocolates. The Apples lived on the east coast of the United States in a small town near New York City. The Chocolate family lived across the Atlantic Ocean on the west coast of Europe in the very small country of Belgium. Although the Apples and the Chocolates lived far away from each other, they had one thing in common—they cared about the Earth.

Benjamin and Michelle Apple lived with their mom and their dog, Cortland. Benjamin was in the sixth grade. He loved to play baseball. Michelle had the most beautiful rock collection of anyone in her fourth-grade class. Both children loved to read. Mrs. Apple owned a company that made products out of plastic.

In school, Benjamin and Michelle learned that the world around them was in trouble. The Earth was running out of acceptable room for all the garbage that was being thrown out.

Their teachers, Ms. Gail and Ms. Robin, taught that one of the ways to help stop this problem was to *recycle*. When something is recycled it is broken down, and then it is taken apart and made into something else so that it is useful once more.

They also learned the word *reuse*. This is when something is used over and over again instead of being thrown away. Reusing things like plastic and paper grocery bags, writing and wrapping paper, and glass containers stops waste and makes less trash.

Ms. Gail and Ms. Robin explained that people are using up too many natural resources, which are special treasures from the Earth. Oil, natural gas, wood, coal, and water are examples of natural resources. Some of these resources are turned into energy. Heat for our homes, gasoline for our cars, oil for making plastic, and electricity are a few ways that natural resources are used. Forgetting to turn off the lights, and letting cars run when it isn't necessary are just two ways that people waste natural resources.

The children learned that the Earth's clean water is also being wasted. Simply taking a short shower instead of a bath saves many gallons of clean water. Turning off the running water while brushing teeth is another water-saving trick.

People must *reduce* their use of the Earth's natural resources. Using less resources now means having more in the future.

Benjamin and Michelle thought a lot about the trouble their planet was in. Since their mom owned a company that made plastic products, the children decided to talk to her about what they had heard.

Michelle said, "Our teachers told us the Earth is running out of space to put trash, and some of this trash is plastic. Why don't you just stop making things out of plastic?"

"That's a good question," Mrs. Apple replied. "The answer is that plastic is a part of everyone's life. Plastic is strong, doesn't rust, and doesn't weigh very much. It has become important in producing hundreds of thousands of items, from life-saving medical products to parts for rockets that go into space. Plastic makes cars lighter so they use up less gas. It is also used as packaging to protect items from getting damaged and spoiled. It provides insulation in houses so that people don't get too cold. Can you think of other ways plastic is used?" The children quickly thought of many products.

Mrs. Apple then continued, "You know, the people who make plastic items have families just like ours. Over the years, these people have worked very hard to improve the quality of plastic. Many plastics made today can be recycled."

"Do you and the other people from plastics companies help the people who recycle?" asked Benjamin.

"Yes," answered their mom. "We work very closely with recycling centers. Together, we turn plastic trash into new plastic products like bottles and containers. Our town's recycling center, where Cousin Emil works, has a very special machine that comes all the way from the country of Belgium. This machine turns plastic trash into plastic lumber called garbo. Garbo is used in some of the same ways wooden lumber is used.

Benjamin and Michelle were proud of their mom. Mrs. Apple said it was time for them to reduce, reuse, and recycle in their own home. It was also time to start purchasing more recycled products.

Mrs. Apple knew her children needed to see what other people were doing to help. First she called her cousin Emil, who ran the town recycling center, to ask for his help. Then she called her children's teachers. Everyone agreed that a field trip to the recycling center was a great idea.

The day of the trip, Cousin Emil met the children and their teachers as they got off the bus.

The first place he took the group was to a huge room that was filled with empty plastic containers of all shapes and sizes. The children saw empty milk and juice bottles, peanut butter jars, soap containers, and egg cartons.

"Wow!" exclaimed Arthur when he saw the huge pile of plastic trash.

"A plastic mountain!" said David, Arthur's twin brother.

Emil and the teachers chuckled at the twins' excitement.

"I know it may be hard for you to believe," said Emil, "but there's treasure hidden in that pile of trash!"

"Pirate treasure?" a fourth grader named Cheryl asked excitedly.

"Well, not exactly," replied Emil. "What I mean is that all that plastic trash will soon be recycled and turned into wonderful things! Come, I'll show you."

Emil went over to the plastic mountain and picked up an empty beverage bottle. He pointed to something at the bottom.

"See this little mark?" asked Emil.

The children nodded.

"It is called a symbol and it tells the people who recycle what kind of plastic the container is made of. There are different symbols for different kinds of plastic."

A little boy named Charlie asked, "Why do recyclers need to know this?"

Emil responded, "Well, it's because some centers only recycle certain kinds of plastic."

"What kind of plastic is recycled here?" asked a red-headed girl named Libby.

"This center recycles all plastic trash."

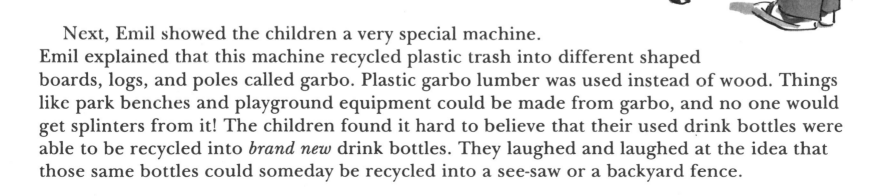

Next, Emil showed the children a very special machine.
Emil explained that this machine recycled plastic trash into different shaped
boards, logs, and poles called garbo. Plastic garbo lumber was used instead of wood. Things
like park benches and playground equipment could be made from garbo, and no one would
get splinters from it! The children found it hard to believe that their used drink bottles were
able to be recycled into *brand new* drink bottles. They laughed and laughed at the idea that
those same bottles could someday be recycled into a see-saw or a backyard fence.

For the children, watching each step of the plastic trash being recycled was like magic.

First, the plastic was loaded onto a moving belt, and it was taken to a shredding machine to be turned into chunks.

Giant magnets passed through the chunks to take out any pieces of metal that might have gotten mixed in with the plastic.

The plastic chunks were put through a grinding machine and turned into tiny plastic chips.

The plastic chips were ready for the garbo machine. Slowly, they were dropped into a funnel at the top of the machine. Next, the chips were heated up and melted.

Once melted, the liquid plastic flowed into different-shaped molds. The molds passed through a water tank to cool the melted plastic.

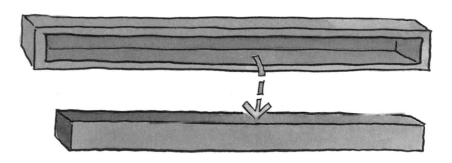

After they had cooled, the new pieces of garbo were taken out of the molds. The plastic trash had been turned into garbo lumber.

Before they left, Emil gave each of the children a small piece of garbo. They thanked him for the garbo and for showing them one way to recycle plastic. They couldn't wait to get home and tell their parents about the recipe for making garbo.

Each year, Mrs. Apple took a few trips because of her work. Soon, she would be joining Cousin Emil on a trip to Europe. They would be going to Brussels, the capital city of Belgium. There they would meet Mr. Chocolate, a friend of Emil's and the inventor of the garbo machine. This time, as a surprise, Mrs. Apple planned to take Benjamin and Michelle along.

The Apple children squealed with delight when they heard about the trip. They jumped up and down when they learned that Mr. Chocolate had two children who were almost the same ages that they were! There was a boy named Robert and a girl named Polly.

Finally, the big day arrived! The airplane ride was very long. It took almost eight hours to get to the city of Brussels.

The Chocolate family was waiting at the airport. Mr. and Mrs. Chocolate greeted Mrs. Apple and Emil with the traditional Belgian hello. They went from cheek to cheek with kisses three times in a row.

Then Robert and Polly said, "Bon jour, American friends!" The Apple children were very happy to hear that their new friends could speak English as well as French.

Benjamin gave Robert a New York baseball cap, and Robert gave Benjamin an official soccer ball. Michelle handed Polly a stuffed toy dog. Polly put a Belgian lace doll into Michelle's arms.

The two families were together every day of the vacation. Michelle and Benjamin noticed the Chocolates also reduced, reused, and recycled. They told Polly and Robert that they did many of the same things in their home.

Mr. Chocolate said to Benjamin and Michelle, "I wish you could come to Belgium in May. That is the month of our Recycling Fair."

"Recycling Fair?" questioned Michelle.

"Yes. All the communities gather together, share ideas, and show new ways that they are helping the environment."

Cousin Emil and the Apple family enjoyed the many wonderful sights of Belgium. They visited beautiful museums and busy fishing villages. They took walks along tree-lined canals. They also saw fine Belgian lace being made, and they enjoyed a grand outdoor puppet show. They even got to see how the garbo machines were put together in Mr.Chocolate's factory.

One day, Mr. Chocolate took Cousin Emil and the Apple family on a picnic. They went to a beautiful park that had once been a run-down lot.

As they walked through the park, Mr. Chocolate explained, "All the garbo used in this park was donated by my company. Using garbo instead of wood means that no trees had to be cut down. Garbo helped save a natural resource!"

Mr. Chocolate continued, "Can you spot the things in this park that are made out of garbo?"

"This"   "That"   "LOTS OF THINGS!"

25

Before they knew it, the trip was over and it was time to leave Belgium. Everyone was very sad on the ride to the airport. Although they were happy to go back home, the Apple children did not want to leave their new friends. They agreed to become "recycling pen pals" and write to each other often—but only on recycled paper.

Once Michelle and Benjamin were home, they told their teachers and friends about their wonderful trip to Belgium. They also talked about the need to do more about recycling. Benjamin and Michelle suggested that the school have a Recycling Fair just like the one Mr. Chocolate had told them about.

"A fair about garbage? What would we have to do?" asked Steven.

Michelle answered, "We can share ideas on ways to reduce, reuse, and recycle."

"This is quite an interesting idea," said Miss Gail. "If you are serious about this, the first thing to do is form a committee to organize and plan the fair."

"Hey, I know," exclaimed Michael, "we can call it the Garb Ed Committee! It would stand for Garbage Education."

"We can invite the whole community to our fair," said Elsie.

"I know," said Audree, "we can reuse pieces of cardboard and make signs to advertise the event."

Mary jumped up. "Let's send special invitations to Mayor Peter and all the people who work at Town Hall."

The children became more excited by the minute. They thought of fun ways to make the fair a success.

"How about a contest?" said Jessica. "All fairs have contests with ribbons for prizes."

"Terrific suggestion!" exclaimed Miss Gail.

Lindsay, Michelle Apple's best friend, raised her hand, "Since it is so important for us to reuse things instead of throwing them away, let's have a Treasure of Trash contest!" Lindsay continued, "A ribbon can be given for the best object made from reused or recycled material."

"What a smart idea!" Miss Robin exclaimed. "This way, all the children will have a chance to create something from trash! Students can work alone, with a partner, or in a group."

The children left school that day with ideas buzzing in their heads.

On the day of the fair, the school was filled with visitors. All the people saw the many ways the children had turned their school into an important place in the community.

A booth was set up by the Can Collectors.

There was a Dirt Diggers display.

The Plastic People were very busy.

And the Paper Partners demonstrated all they had learned.

The cafeteria was filled with the students' contest entries. The room had become a wonderland of "treasures." Choosing the contest winner was going to be very hard.

Mary May proudly stood beside her poem, The Treasure of Trash.

Finally, the time had come to announce the contest winners. Everyone was asked to go to the auditorium.

Ms. Gail, Ms. Robin, and Principal Donald walked on stage. Ms. Gail said, "Thank you for coming to our school's first recycling fair. We would like to praise all of the children who have worked so hard to make our fair a success. We hope this will be the first of many fairs to bring the people of our community together to work toward a cleaner, healthier, safer environment."

"The time has now come to announce the winner," Principal Donald said as he opened the envelope and pulled out a sheet of recycled paper.

"For this year's contest, we have co-winners! I would like to call Benjamin and Michelle Apple up on stage."

Applause filled the air. Students and visitors jumped to their feet and cheered for Benjamin and Michelle as they made their way to the stage. The curtains opened and the audience saw the winning "treasure." It was a doghouse for Cortland, and it had been made out of garbo logs. A pillow filled with shredded plastic chips was inside the doghouse.

Ms. Robin turned to the Apple children and said, "And now for your prize ribbons."

Suddenly, the doors in the back of the auditorium swung open. There stood Robert and Polly Chocolate! They were holding the prize ribbons. Benjamin and Michelle couldn't believe their eyes! Was it really true? Were their friends from Belgium really there?

Polly and Robert ran up on the stage and hugged their two American friends. They were all laughing and hugging each other at the same time. Everyone felt like they were in a dream. A wonderful, happy dream.

That night, the Chocolates, the Apples, and Cousin Emil were together. The grown-ups talked about how proud they were of the children, who had taught so many people to reduce, reuse, and recycle. Now everyone knew how trash could be a treasure!

While Cortland slept in his new recycled home, the children made a promise to be friends always.

About the Authors

Linda Mandel and Hedi Michelle Mandel are mother-daughter co-authors and the best of friends.

Hedi has been a New Yorker most of her life. She attended the University of Maryland College Park and received a B.S. in marketing from the College of Business and Management. For three years, she worked as Vice President of Sales Link, Inc., a family business that represents manufacturers of plastics. Presently, Hedi works for the Elizabeth Arden Company in Product Development. In her spare time, Hedi enjoys exercising, reading, playing tennis, bicycling, collecting unusual dolls, and spending time with family and friends. After her marriage in June, she plans to reside in New York City.

Linda is a born and bred New Yorker. She is the mother of Hedi and a son, Steven. Linda graduated from St. Thomas Aquinas College in Sparkhill, New York, with a B.S. in business administration. Her past work experiences include a stint as a newspaper reporter and managing a plastics manufacturing plant. Linda is now President of Sales Link, Inc., as well as Ink Link, the book division. Her free time is spent fund-raising for Ronald McDonald House charities, cross-country skiing, playing tennis, aerobic exercising, bicycling, reading, and writing poetry.

The idea for *The Treasure of Trash: A Recycling Story* was born while attending a recycling conference in 1990. Linda and Hedi are presently researching the second book in their children's recycling series.

About the Illustrator

Dick Codor's cartoons and drawings appear regularly in *Crain's New York Business*, *Hadassah Magazine*, and other periodicals. He is the illustrator of the perennial best-seller *The Big Book of Jewish Humor*, as well as a number of children's books. Born and raised in Delaware, Dick has lived in San Francisco and Jerusalem. He now lives with his family in Brooklyn, New York, where he is personally responsible for taking out the trash.